Many-Storied House

Many-Storied House

Poems

George Ella Lyon

UNIVERSITY PRESS OF KENTUCKY

Published by the University Press of Kentucky
Scholarly publisher for the Commonwealth,
serving Bellarmine University, Berea College, Centre
College of Kentucky, Eastern Kentucky University,
The Filson Historical Society, Georgetown College,
Kentucky Historical Society, Kentucky State University,
Morehead State University, Murray State University,
Northern Kentucky University, Transylvania University,
University of Kentucky, University of Louisville,
and Western Kentucky University.
All rights reserved.

Editorial and Sales Offices: The University Press of Kentucky
663 South Limestone Street, Lexington, Kentucky 40508-4008
www.kentuckypress.com

17 16 15 14 13   5 4 3 2 1

Library of Congress Cataloging-in-Publication Data
Lyon, George Ella, 1949-
 [Poems. Selections]
 Many-storied house : poems / George Ella Lyon.
   pages ; cm. — (Kentucky voices)
 Includes index.
 ISBN 978-0-8131-4261-6 (pbk. : alk. paper) —
 ISBN 978-0-8131-4276-0 (epub) — ISBN 978-0-8131-4277-7 (pdf)
 I. Title.
 PS3562.Y4454A6 2013
 811'.54—dc23
                        2013015477

This book is printed on acid-free paper meeting
the requirements of the American National Standard
for Permanence in Paper for Printed Library Materials.

Manufactured in the United States of America.

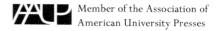 Member of the Association of
American University Presses

Deep in the house is the carpenter's hand
beginning things at their end

Contents

Kitchen

Basement

Garage

Flood

Upstairs

Stairway

Library

Hall

My Room

Brother's Room

Parents' Room

Many-Storied House

Provenance

Here I stand, at the beginning
with more questions than
answers.
   What I know is Papaw
built the house I grew up in,
at Rio Vista, which is down
below Loyall, four miles from
Harlan, the county seat. It's
on First Street, #108, I found
out when we sold it. Fourth
house on the right, two-story,
reddish brown and white.
You can't miss it.

Downstairs

Porch

Dining Room   Kitchen   New Room

Living Room

Hall

Hall
Closet   Bath

Porch

First Floor

Door

we passed
will pass
are passing
through

threshold
of our
threshing
holding

lintel
of embraces

portal
of goodbyes

our DNA
clasping
your
handle

Bathroom

This is the window
they put a kid through
when they lock their keys
in the house. It was
my brother till he got
too big, then my wiry
cousin David, then me.

No screen or storm window,
so once they haul up
the sash, somebody (not
Daddy because of
his back) puts hands on
both sides of your waist
and lifts you straight up
like a post hole digger,
then eases you through
the slot. Your task is
to find the linoleum
with your Keds, steady
yourself, go out the
bathroom door—avoiding
the scary faces in
the varnished pine—
step into the hall,

turn the latch left (that's
toward the train track),
and let your keepers
back in the zoo.

Closet

Just inside the door,
a closet to your left holds
umbrella stand, folding chairs,
coat rack, and amiable shelf

for games and puzzles. Unlike
ones in the rest of the house,
these games have directions,
a board so you can see where

you are, written rules saying
when they are over. Likewise,
the puzzles have pictures on
top so you know where

the edges are and what scene
you are trying to fit together.

Passage

The morning Daddy was leaving
for the surgery that would not save him
the doorbell rang and he opened
to a jaunty man on the front porch,
a familiar cadger who never paid back
a loan. Tired of lies, Daddy refused
and both men turned away. But a hinge
in his heart turned Daddy back. "I'll
give it to you," he said. It was the last
thing the world asked of him and he gave.

That Chair

She almost died in that wingback
            chair by the living room window.

We'd eaten at Mount Aire up on Pine
            Mountain—a Sunday in September, it was—

when pain began to twist her heart
            as we whip-stitched those switchback curves

coming down. She said nothing. This
            was an anniversary celebration for my

other grandparents. She said nothing
            when the car drew up to the house, just

got out, traveled driveway and steps,
            threshold and hall, walked across

the living room to that chair. Then it
            was obvious, sweat pouring off, her

face all the wrong color, her eyes blank.
            Someone ran for Flora, our neighbor,

a nurse, who sent my mother for the bottle
            of ammonia under the sink. She twisted

the cap off, then held Granny Buby's head,
                    forcing her, if she was breathing

to breathe that jolt. After the ambulance
                    and my parents left, Flora told me

my grandmother's corset, which bound
                    her middle tight as roads bound that

mountain, was the other savior. "It kept
                    enough blood in her heart," Flora said.

"If it had pooled in her feet, she'd be gone."
                    I think of this when I sit in that chair

my grandmother didn't die in. No
                    wings on her back that day.

Art

When Daddy got the hi-fi,
which replaced the Crosley radio
just inside the living room door,
it came with a demonstration record
to show what "rich lifelike sound"
Magnavox could bring into your home.

Our neighborhood was bound
by mountains, river, railroad.
Coal trains whistled, rattling
our walls day and night. But

when Daddy turned on that
hi-fi and the needle rode
the black platter, we called
the neighbors. "You've got
to come hear this," we said,
thrilled at the *whooo* and *hiss*
and roar of a "real train" so close.

Visitor

That man, that shining man—
    grackle-black hair, bedazzling eyes,
    a voice like effervescent velvet
sitting on the rose couch
strumming a guitar—a guitar!—
and singing
    Once a jolly swagman
    camped by a billabong
    under the shade
    of a Coolibah tree
his Australian mouth kissing
strange words into song.

Why, he was an adult and alive!
happy as a kid, I could tell,
with my ten-year-old knowing,
and this was sweeter than the blackberry
cobbler Mother had served in his honor.
Right there, that night, Desmond Tease
waltzed my sky with a whole new
matilda of stars.

Money Laundering

Because Daddy's dry cleaners
had been broken into
and the safe busted up
to get the day's take,
which was less
than the cost of repairing
the safe and the door,
Daddy took to bringing the money
bag home and leaving the safe
open. Because we didn't have
a safe at home and because
that seemed a stupid place
to keep money anyway
Daddy put it in the washer.
So eventually it got washed.
Bills and coins and checks
dancing around the agitator
(in the bag of course),
going into spin.
            And because
you cannot tender wet cash
at the bank, Daddy laid it all out
on the dining room table to dry.
Neighbors dropped in
for an evening cup of coffee
served in the living room
with apple pie and a clear view
of that table with its banquet

of Jackson-Lincoln-Washington-
Jefferson laid out. Silent word
went through the family: pretend
it's not there. And silent signals
slipped from guest to guest:
Do you see what I see? Do you
think they print it in the basement?
I swear, it doesn't even look *dry*.

Oh, My

The house inside our house
is a gingerbread house
and it is on the dining room table.

There is no house inside the gingerbread
house probably, but you don't know.
You can't see in the gingerbread windows

outlined in icing with sugar wafer shutters,
so you don't know, do you, that there aren't
gingerbread people in there who have made

a miniature version of this house
you are standing in out of whatever
gingerbread people eat, which surely

is not gingerbread. Perhaps they
bake little boards, melt sugar into glass
windows, cut chewy shingles out of licorice

with a paring knife. And if this is true,
then it wasn't a dream, that raisin eye,
huge and puckered, that I saw peering

through the window
yesterday morning
to see if we exist.

Ritual

Home from work
Daddy shucks

the leather-sheathed
back brace that

straps down his pain
so he can stand.

He rolls dented
shoulders, rests

the brace against
the china cabinet.

Collector's Item

On the cornice board
above the window
is a large plate painted
with a brown and amber
pheasant against a jade
and spring-green ground.

It belonged to Ella Ezelle
Lane Culwell, my mother's
mother's mother, the woman
who was kind to her, the one
who, widowed, with three
small children, started
a boarding house, married
a boarder, made it to Memphis
from the dirt roads of Prescott
(still unpaved in 1972).

I know my great-grandmother
from one picture,
delectable descriptions
of her salmon salad,
her bold signature in a second
edition of Swinburne,
this great plate, and the way
her hand, calm at the small
of my mother's back,
steadied us.

Phone

This is where she stood
when she took the call
that November morning.

"Mother," I said
from my hospital bed,
"The baby is here!"

"Who is this?" she asked,
an edge to her voice.

"Mother, it's me. I've had
the baby—" "Who? Who
did you say is calling?"

"Your daughter! Joey—
he was born
early this morning."

"All right. I have to go.
Your daddy's not doing
well at all."

August 4, 1944

My brother turns two, talking a blue streak.
Hot as it is, Mother bakes a cake, invites
the grandparents down. First there's
spaghetti, which the toddler eats delicately
by fistfuls. Then the shiny chocolate
temple of cake. Everyone crowds around,
singing to the future.

                    To the future
they have pledged themselves, eight people
hiding on the other side of the world. Then
this day the bookcase is swung back, stairway
revealed. With shouts and shoves they are
herded out at gunpoint. All but one will
fall to the Final Solution. But the Gestapo
won't find the teenage girl's birthday gift,
a red-and-white checked diary. The world
will find that.

Reveille

Standing
On the white metal table
In my mother's blue kitchen
Just turned twelve and full of joy
My brother puts the cold gold
Of the trumpet to his lips
And blasts the house
Awake.

Blood and Water

When Mother came home from the hospital
with my brother, her firstborn, Daddy's

mother brought scrumptious homemade
meals (Swiss steak, mashed potatoes

and gravy; fried chicken, greens, and corn
on the cob) so the new mother could

focus on the baby while she regained her
strength. But Jo only brought one plate.

She was feeding her boy, not that Fowler girl.

The Radio

that melted
          onto the toaster oven
when someone baked a potato at Christmas

should have been on the counter between
the coffee pot and canisters but got moved
to the toaster oven due to an influx
of stack cake, fruitcake, and peanut butter roll.

That radio gave us, on Saturdays all year long,
The Birthday Club brought to you by Mosely Safes
and McCaskey Cash Registers.
                              I loved those names:
Mosely Safes sounds like a cashmere scarf wound
around your neck. And *McCaskey Cash Registers*
makes your mouth do something between chewing
and whistling.

                    Oh, birthday greetings were rich:
"Elmer says 'You're the best!' to Rita on her fortieth"
or "You made us Mom and Dad. Happy first ever,
Jimmy Saylor!" But I relished the brand names
of office equipment, just as deep in the season
of sweets, I hungered for beets, collards, soup
beans, and cornbread, Jo's odoriferous turnip stew.

Legacy

When they were tearing down the Bank of Harlan,
somebody called Daddy to say he should come
empty Papaw's safety deposit box. Papaw
had been dead for years and this was the first
anyone had heard of his private hidey hole.

Home from college, I was at the table that night
when Daddy laid out the contents: a deed, a poem,
a packet of Papaw's love letters to Jo, and a pistol.
All were spread on the table amid the remains
of pork chops, biscuits, and gravy when the doorbell
rang and I got up to answer. Friends, not close ones,
happened to be in our neighborhood and stopped by.

I ushered them down the hall to the kitchen where
Mother had slipped the pistol off the table and under
her apron. Daddy carried in chairs while I cleared
the dishes, put on more coffee, passed a plate
of Lorna Doones. Poem, deed, letters lay
unmentioned while visitors munched, and my pistol-
packing mama sat frozen with that heat in her lap.

Junk Drawer

It held Boy Scout knives
and the innards of kites,
old church bulletins, oilcloth
for picnics, whistles, yoyos,
a Worldwide Offering Box,
a black ceramic fur-tipped
poodle from the set Daddy
gave away at the cleaners,
a toy bow and half an arrow,
the front page from V-E Day,
a dried-up shoeshine kit,
and net left over from my
kindergarten graduation dress.
Junk is junk, that's the great
thing about it. All this except
the newspaper could go,
but the newspaper would go
with it. Junk is the Secret
Service protecting what is
precious. It slows down
traffic between this world
and the next.

Vision

I was old enough to help carry in groceries, lift them from the chuffy paper sacks, and put them away. Cold things first: milk on the top shelf, meat on the bottom, celery and carrots in the crisper. Mounding fruit in a bowl on the counter, Mother said, "You want to see something no one has ever seen before?" "No one?" I echoed. "No one," she said again. "Sure," I replied. "Where do we go?"

Mother laughed, reached for the cutting board, palmed an orange, opened the drawer, and drew out a knife. She halved the fruit. Citrus incense rose in the coffee-rich kitchen. "Right here," she said, gesturing with the blade at the orange's cathedral window.

Over Coffee

"I think if I'd been a man," Mother told me,
"I would have played football for Notre Dame."
She was eighty-eight when she said this.

She could have done it, too, followed by Harvard Law
and clerking for the Supreme Court. As it was, she had
us—family and house, PTA and Heart Fund—till my brother
went to college. Then she ran the Chamber of Commerce

from 1961 until she died. I think if *I'd* been a man,
she'd never have sat at that table and told me all those stories,
how her mother hit her with the butcher knife but only
the dull side, how she slapped her so hard it bloodied
her nose. Mother needed to see her pain reflected
in my face so she could push it away. What do
you think *you'd* have done, she'd say angrily,
with seven little children, your husband
gone all week, and you living
at the back door
of nowhere?

Daddy's Last Christmas

He plays the board game
"By Jove!" with his grandsons

in the kitchen. His mother just
buried, he is dense with grief

in the photo that I snapped.

The boys, lithe and limber, lean
over the mythic board, while he

pulls back, knowing the dice
are not in his hands.

Kitchen Table

This table stands where
the green table stood
where they played Scrabble
with the Babbages, wrote out
statements for Nu-Way Cleaners,
where Mother made out rolls
and we sculpted Christmas
candles and she tightened
the vise on the cast-iron grinder
that turned ham scraps to
ham salad. This table
where she made calls
for the March of Dimes
and for the Chamber,
where she said I was
treating her like a child
where I said I was only
trying to take care of her.
This table stands
where the white enameled
table stood on which she
mixed the formula for our
bottles, before the table
we antiqued that got carried
away by the flood. This table
is where she opened
the newspaper to Daddy's photo:
Harlan Businessman Dead at 68.
This is where she sat down and howled.

What Won't Burn

When I opened
the cast-iron door
of the furnace
on New Year's Eve

and leaned
over the cinder pile
to drop my diary
in the flames

I was thirteen—
thought guilt
and shame
could burn

like red leatherette
and small
white pages.
I didn't know

they outlasted
conflagration
like the diary's
charred metal

lock.

Bucket Brigade

Colossal storms

        came after Christmas

rolling off hillsides

        rising in rivers

furious water

        holding us flood-fast

radio-riveted

        ready to run.

We stood on the steps

        to the sloshy basement

watched the water

        work its way up.

"Get buckets! Bail!"

        somebody bellowed.

So for an hour

        we hauled our hearts

in pots and pans

        pouring our fear

down the toilet

        draining danger

right to the river.

        At last we reckoned

or some sense

        seized us:

what work was worse

       or could be weaker

than flushing a flood

       to a fiendish river?

Somebody sighed

       and started the coffee.

Two a.m.

       but time was in tatters.

"What comes will come,"

       we said, compliant,

while slowly the wearisome

       water went down.

The Ham

Every fall, when maple blood was drying,
my father hung a ham in the garage—
country-salted, curing for the Fourth—
between two racks of clothes we didn't want.

Some nights they'd send me there to rob the freezer
of blueberries or glistening slabs of cake.
By freezerlight I'd watch green shelves appearing,
their tenants warped and moldy from the damp:
entire works of James Whitcomb Riley,
jigsaw puzzles—*Holland, Lake Louise,*—
spiral handles of white graveyard baskets,
a Signet classic, *Love without Fear.*

But sometimes I would stop, lulled by the stillness,
perhaps to see the porchlight through the door,
and catch sight of the ham among the coatsleeves—
sudden gleaming flesh that was all wound.
I'd leap the stairs, slamming doors and light
against the deadweight heart that stopped the house.

New Room

When I first saw Daddy in the ICU,
still on a respirator, he motioned
for a notepad and wrote, under-
lining each word:

Prince Edward Island

He meant to go there. And that
imagining was the healthiest
he ever got. He went downhill
for a month until doctors, claiming
success, sent him home to die.

Then the new room, made from
our old garage, meant for an office,
was perfect for his sickroom.
Just six steps down from the kitchen—
more than Daddy could manage
but few enough so Mother was never
far away. She or my brother could
help him to the bathroom.

He hadn't spoken in a while. Words
were leaving, like the power
to swallow, like any desire to
go on. Yet one day Daddy appeared
in the kitchen doorway—too weak

and wobbly for the journey
he'd just made. "I didn't come this far,"
he said, "to be separated from you,"
and sat down at his table for the last time.

Flood

It Got Us This Time

Cusp of spring after the winter
they converted from coal to oil.
Ground frozen, so the tank
nests in the basement.
Snow   snow   snow
slopes, valleys thick with it.
Then, at the birth of April,
rain in torrents.

Strip-mine benches, clear-cut hills can't hold it.
Cumberland River, coal-silted, can't either.
On and on water comes   over roads
up basement steps   under front door
through windows   River rising in the house

Daddy gone to town
to save Jo and his business.
Mother sick but carrying
all she can upstairs
then heading for higher ground.

From Bailey's Loop
above the railroad
she watches Rio Vista fill
like a sinkful of dirty dishes

Next day when rain stops
and nature pulls the plug

they go home
to find what everybody finds:
no heat, light, water
just flood mud and ruin

and for them, something else:
oil—the sick slick of it—
smearing everything.
River   had cracked that tank
against the joists
                                    like an egg.

No Light

As if to pay
for all it took
the river left

in the middle of the living room floor

a miner's
orange
hardhat.

Worst Flood in Harlan County History

from Daddy's journal
April 4, 1977

Gladys stayed home—had something like flu. It had been rain-
ing HARD ALL DAY SUNDAY AND SUNDAY NIGHT. River up
and nearly over road at Jones' Motel and Noe's BBQ. Went down
to Jo—told her that there could be a flood probably worse than
1963. Talked to Jim—he said pull all switches—forget motors in
all properties. Elmer tried to get to L&N railroad track to walk
medicine to Gladys—couldn't get there. Jim's mother used same
prescription. Took it across mountain at Airport Road and walked
it to her.

By 3 p.m. Hoskins Bldg., State Mine Bureau, Carr Bldg, IRS
all flooded. Wallace came down to help me move records of Har-
lan Federal up high. Water started coming in there at 5:30 p.m.
No telephone contact with Jo or Gladys. Could talk to Jim. Joined
Charlie Bissell in flood watch. Ed Hatmaker brought sandwiches
and coffee. Flood is behind Bissell's.

We now know that all of Loyall and Rio Vista flooded. That
takes in our house. Many people are homeless. Damage WILL BE
VERY HIGH. Charlie Bissell stayed with Ed. I stayed with Wallace.
Was told that Gladys was on hill above Rio Vista at Mrs. Nannie
Rowland's son-in-law's. Tried to phone but couldn't get through.
Did get Jo on Irene Richardson phone. She's OK. Flood over her
dining room table.

Wallace and I back downtown at 10:30 p.m. Flood crested at this time. It got into the back of the Harlan National Bank, under the red light at the corner of Central and Main.

Interim

from Daddy's journal
Saturday, May 14, 1977

Our HUD trailer
placed in location
between our home

and Mrs. Rowland.
We will move in
when hooked up.

Unknown as to
how long we
will live there.

Threshold

They were determined to have
their New Year's Eve party
at home, hell and high
water having already come.
"Bring a chair," they told
friends, since they hadn't
moved in yet. The empty
house was beautiful: new
walls, bare floors shining,
card table in the kitchen,
lit by a hurricane lamp.

"How high did it get, Bob?"
Wallace asked, his hill
house having stayed dry.
Daddy put his hand above
the kitchen radiator.
"Up to here. That's the magic
line." A chorus of "Yes sir,
the magic line," and "It got
higher than that in my house."

Come midnight, this crew
found the usual toast
not enough. Out the front
door they went, to stand
around the McPherons'
blue spruce, its deep boughs

threaded with colored light.
Hands linked, they sang, "We'll
take a cup o' kindness yet,"
then went back in and did.

Upstairs

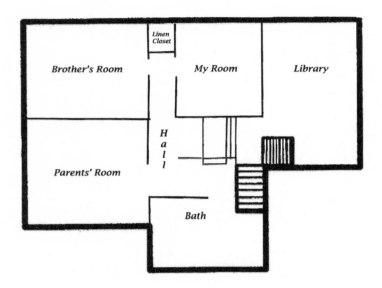

Second Floor

Landing

This square where I sneakily sat
to watch TV through the library's

glass door long after my bedtime,
where I once gave myself away

singing "The Star-Spangled Banner"
as WATE signed off, this square

was sometimes Perry Mason's
helicopter and sometimes Mt. Sinai,

down from which Moses strode when
we played *The Ten Commandments*.

Now it's the place where I stand
hands out behind my mother

to help her navigate
the last two steps.

On Those Shelves

From the landing you step
down into a room
out over the garage:

This is the room that made us who we were:
book lovers, scholars, people of the word,
who found a safe place between hard covers.
Deckle- or gilt-edged, the wild world opened:
story, knowledge, emotion we'd been taught
to hold in.

On those shelves Papaw built
into the wall below the windows
stood the many mansions of our house.

Interior Design

My mother decided
my father never noticed
anything in the house.

To prove her point, she
bought a packet of the plastic
clay you use to hang posters

and stuck a few items
on the library wall
above the couch: a match

box, Wite-Out, a Kleenex
pack: feather-weight
things. He said nothing.

"See?" she told me, and stuck
up an artificial rose
and nail scissors. No

response. "Unbelievable,"
she said, adding Scotch Tape,
pipe cleaners, brush rollers,

one of the coin purses
the cleaners gave away.
Daddy just walked to his chair

every night, dozing off
halfway through the news.
Finally, when the wall looked

as though the plaster had
broken out in junk, Mother
took it all down. "It's

hopeless," she told me.
But that night, Daddy said,
"You know, I usually

like the way you decorate
but that didn't look
quite right."

Portrait

In the library above the couch
hung a portrait of the house
painted by Robert Easley
who lived down on Fifth Street.
It was done when the house
was younger, when the garage
was the garage and boxwoods
guarded the porch.
      Of course
I wondered if, on the inside,
in saltbox fashion
the library wall held
a tiny painting of the house
and so forth. Old enough to know
this wasn't true—paint was paint—
I wondered anyway. Maybe because
of the deer in the linen closet. Maybe
because I knew that for its family,
a house is mostly what you cannot see.

Facing the windows above
the bookshelves, the portrait
looked out its own windows
twice. In its acrylic front yard
the dogwood always bloomed,
the fullest season still ahead.

Smithereens

October and we're in the library
watching the president on TV.
Standing up to the Russians putting
missiles in Cuba. October and I
am in the eighth grade, old enough to know
the shift in the charge of the room is not
a whiff of thunderstorm, that the stunned
look on my parents' faces is fear.

The gray and white gravity of JFK
leaks out into the house, dims scarlet
dogwood in the front yard, yellow
Dutch elm in the back. It takes the taste
of meatloaf too. The drain we could all
go down is whirling at our feet.

On the dusty blackboard last year,
Mr. Smith looped the invisible solar
system of the atom. "The energy
that holds everything together can
be reversed," he said, "and blow it all
apart." Some schools had bomb drills,
kids cowering under their useless desks,
but we didn't—the teacher explained—
because we lived so close to Oak Ridge.
I was relieved till walking home it hit me
what she meant: Oak Ridge was a prime

target. "No need to worry" = "No hope."
What was wrong with grownups?

At least the president, the youngest ever,
with a yacht, a glossy wife, and kids
coloring in the Oval Office, at least
he was telling the truth: This is what
the world is. Great forces must stick to
their orbits or unleash the rush that will
blow us all to smithereens.

Memory Book

I'd found the album on a shelf behind
the TV among coin books, stacks of *Life*
and *Look,* my brother's map collection.
I was exploring, not snooping. Or so
I thought. Until the last page, this was
a book about life, about friends:
giddy girls, skinny, leggy, laughing.
Mickey inscribed in white ink on each
black page, and beneath the photos:
*at Martha's, at school, with the Suzy-Q
Club.* No way to know who she was,

why we had this book. Then came a shot
of her standing with my grandmother, right
on that sidewalk I walked every Sunday
of my life. *Mickey and Mrs. Fowler.*
Granny Buby held a broom. They'd stopped
her in her work. Why would this Mickey
be at my grandparents' house? Then
the final page, a newspaper clipping:
LOCAL TEEN KILLED. MILDRED
HELEN FOWLER, daughter of, sister of,
on her way home from . . .

Knowledge knifed my throat and a sob
rose just as Mother's shadow fell across
the page. "What are you doing? Give me that!"

She tore the book from my grasp. "Don't you
ever touch it again! Do you hear me?"

She could not say,
"Oh, honey, Mickey was my little sister.
Her best friends made this book.
You're old enough now. Let me tell you
about her." Still trying to protect
that girl no one could save,
she could not
let her go, let me in.

It Was a Year

after your daddy died,
she said ten years later,

I was sixty-seven
and I told myself
You have your work,
your family. Are you
going to make something

of what's left or are you
going to lie down and die?

This Is

the chair the husband
and wife emergency team
strapped Mother in to carry
her down from the library
and out to the ambulance.

This is the couch where
she couldn't breathe but
said she would not go
to the hospital.
                This
is the phone where
I called for help, took
things into my hands.

Shit

At eighty-six, recovering from *C. diff,*
my mother tells me somebody said
the S word in front of her.
"I can think of no occasion," she declares,
"when such language is necessary."

"I can," I say. "There are times when that
is the perfect word." Like when you're expected
to eat it, I think. Or when someone's is dumped
on you. Or when you have to get yours together.
Or when your mother's is on the carpet, the couch,
the floor, the bed, the nightclothes. When it's alive
with infection, and you're the one on your knees
cleaning it up.

[Untitled]

Mother? Dead? Who will
tell us what things mean if the
dictionary dies?

By the Laundry Hamper

Something happened
I tell my mother
I am five
That boy across the street
he did something
Something that hurt

He stood above me
saying BAD
BAD, You are BAD
If you tell
they won't believe you
They won't want you
anymore

I ran away
but he trapped me
in a room off the garage
He hurt me harder
Here I say

Something happened
Bad I can't go back there

My mother sorts dirty clothes
She does not touch me

You know that's not true
she says

These are our neighbors
These are our friends
Nothing happened

Linen Closet

What I feared in
the linen closet
was the stupendous
body, long legs, and
driving hooves of
the stag, the flag
of its tail somehow
wedged among
bedsheets. Its
head poked through
the linen closet
wall into my brother's
room, eyes glass,
antlers empty
as a February
tree. I never
looked, of course, in
the linen closet,
so scared was I
of the dead power
of that deer. I
never told my
fear since this fact
fit with mysteries
we accepted: Jesus
on the cross, the deer
trapped in the wall.

Toy Chest

Betty the Beautiful Bride is shut inside.

Dixon, Tiny Tears, Mabel Baby, too.
The bubble stuff I got when I got the flu.

My Snow White coloring book, old orange peel,
my gray View-Master with its picture wheel.

Jump rope, tambourine, pail for sand,
comic book, magazine, little cake pan,

paper dolls whose blond hair feels fake real,
plastic handcuffs and a crashmobile.

Hiding

Mother says we are going across the street
for supper I must come out of the closet
right now I must stop making up stories
I must straighten up and fly right
Nothing to be afraid of
She is warning me
1   2   3

Doll Mother

Papaw made me
a little yellow rocking chair.
I used to put my Dixon doll in it
and rock her so hard and fast
she flew out. That's the kind
of doll mother I was.

I chopped off
my momma doll's hair
in such fashion that she went
from '50s housewife to future
punk—snip-snip.

I wasn't interested
in their clothes as much
as the drama of their lives
—when Ethel's rubbery skin split
and the stuffing foamed out,
—when Dixon's arm popped off,
revealing a cardboard circle
and grommet for a shoulder
—when Mabel Baby's motion-made
Ma-Ma got stuck at *Ma*.

I flourished as the doctor
who patched up their
afflictions, or the mother
who rocked them raucously
in spite of it all.

Night of the Mysteries

1.
It's April
and I've just turned eleven
one spring night
when pain wakes me.
I get up and see blood
in the bed.

Shaking I wake
my mother
who says it's nothing.
She fishes in a drawer
for an elastic contraption
then takes a bandage
from a turquoise
box I have seen
in her closet.

In the bathroom
she threads thin ends
of the Kotex
through the fastener
then has me take off
my clown pajama bottoms
and step into the future.

She can't say
this is nature's

way of preparing
you to have a baby
someday. She can't say
welcome to the mystery.
She can't even say
this will happen again
every month in fact
until you are older
than I am. No one
gave her the words.
She just says "It's all
right. Go to bed.
You'll feel better
in the morning."

2.
I can't sleep,
the sheet cold and wet,
the center of me
knotting and throbbing.
I get up and take a towel
from the bathroom cupboard.
I spread it out and climb back
in, bolt awake. This isn't
my body. It isn't. That's
why it hurts.
            And why isn't
Mother worried? If my
brother woke up bleeding,
I think, she would call
Dr. Foley, who would tell her

to meet him at the hospital
or who'd come by in the morning
with his black bag and pills.
(I am right about this, but not
for any reason I can imagine.)

3.
Cold with fear, hot with pain
I go back to Mother's
bedside. In the smoky
room, radio voices
splinter into
static. Daddy rolls
over, interrupting
a snore. Mother
opens her eyes. "You're
growing up, " she says.
"Take two aspirins
and come get in bed
with us." I do. That's
the worst. She
puts me in between
where once perhaps
was comfort, but now
shame is red
clotted with jewels
and I am trapped
in my body
in their bed.

Off Limits

my brother's room
because of the golden gun
when I was three and he was ten

because of the barbells
when I was six and he was thirteen

and when I was eight
because of the shortwave radio
he and Daddy built in the basement

and when he was eighteen
because he was gone.

How It Smelled

Cap gun
orange peel
valve oil
bar bells
boy.

Sleepless

That night in a froth of wrath
at mother's refusal of the care
I had set up for her, I couldn't sleep.
I was leaving the next day. Was I
leaving the next day? How could I
leave if she wouldn't . . . ? How would I
if she didn't . . . ? Things were fine
as long as the caretaker was me,
that's what she was saying. Then
it was like a visit until she could
go back to work. But help? No.
She didn't need help. I had no
idea how awful I made her feel. No
idea. Calling people on the phone,
setting up interviews. She couldn't
endure another person in her house!
Never mind my life and work
three hours away. I wanted to rip
something to shreds but had no paper.
That's how far from myself I was.
Staying in my brother's room, only
a wall between her head and mine
so I could bolt awake if she called,
I didn't want to wake her, creeping
about the house, have her cough
and ask "What are you doing up?"
so I opened the chest of drawers.
Surely I would find some paper. . . .

Indeed I did: my parents' wedding
announcement and Papaw's death
certificate. Chastened by a cosmic hand
I got in bed and snapped off the light.

Arthritis, 1952

It's like the spell cast on the castle
when Beauty goes to sleep.
Daddy bedfast. Me three years old.
I won't eat unless Mother brings my meal
up to the bedroom with his. I am scared
still. My strong, happy daddy can't walk.
He tries to smile at me. "How we doing,
Sugar?" he asks. I say, "Fine, Daddy," but he
is the answer to that question and he is not
fine. He is terrified, I realize now.
Thirty-five years old, a wife and two children,
and one day, an electrified spine. Stand up
and the pain is beyond beyond, each
nerve a sizzling wire. He is going
by ambulance to Knoxville but I don't
know this. He is going to have his spine
fused. Radiation, bonded with dry-
cleaning chemicals, far down the road
will start his cancer dance. But for now
it will cage the pain. It will lift him from
this bed, wed him to a leather and canvas
brace, send him back to Nu-Way. Once
Daddy can move, the house will wake,
his kingdom shake itself and go on.

The Photo of Granny Buby

corseted and scowling
in a gold frame stands
on my mother's dresser
where every morning
she sits down
to put on her face.

I can't imagine
how she goes out in the world
marked with that look
from a woman
who wouldn't climb the stairs
to help when she hemorrhaged
or lift a finger
to arrange a flower
for her wedding.
She and her daddy did that.

Why she faces
that face
every morning
I cannot comprehend
unless it's to say
Even you
could not
stop me

but when
after almost dying
she came home
from a tour of hospitals
and found the ornaments in her room
had been removed for cleaning
the first thing she carried back
to put her world to rights
was that picture.

November 21, 1963

When they woke
that morning

Daddy asked Mother
if she had heard

on radio news
that the president

had been shot.
"You had a bad

dream," she said.
"He's gone to Dallas."

Half

Everywhere was where
he wasn't
Every breath one more
he didn't take
His place at the table
his chair in the library
his side of the bed
empty
his clothes carried out
given away
his office cleared
his shaving things tossed
with fury and tears
into the trash.
What am I supposed to *do*
with this? she said
over and over, *this*
being the stuff
of grief.

She put her hands on it.
She weeded it out.
No more Bob and Gladys.
No Bob.
Just a world brim with graves
everything steps into.
Just death's hand closed
on the spine
of half your life.

With a Song in His Heart

Daddy called the Walkman
his play-pretty and he loved it

like he loved the radio
that sang him to sleep.

(Mother listened to talk
shows. They had

pillow speakers.) He loved
the radio like he loved

the hi-fi with Mario Lanza's
heart breaking in his voice

or the Beatles looping "Let
It Be" on the eight-track

like he loved my brother
always at the spinet and later

the grand piano striking
heart-sparks from Rachmaninoff

or "Rock of Ages" or giving us
cascading "Autumn Leaves"

the way he loved to drive
around just him and me

Sunday afternoons singing
"Barbara Allen." In that

scarlet town where I was
born, music was our dwelling.

O Daddy, I am leaning
on those everlasting arms.

Sanctus

On Daddy's only morning home,
he had to himself
the full upstairs bathroom
with glossy black tiles
drawn into the plaster
halfway up the wall.
All the rest, and the ceiling,
heaven-blue. Between onyx
and sky, a paper border—
pink swans processing—
from just under the light switch
into the lavatory nook
out and back to the tub
around and back to the toilet
and thus to the door.

Among all this splendor
    Daddy bathed
while we sang "Holy, Holy, Holy"
    he shaved
while we called on
our Father in heaven
He lifted the stopper
on the Old Spice bottle
then poured some in the palm
    of his plump hand
to complete his ablutions

while beneath him in the kitchen
in a slow oven
a slab of roast simmered into dinner

and four miles away
trousered and crinolined
the rest of us
were washed in the blood of the Lamb.

Company

How could a child,
the last-born
of the last-born
of my mother's far-
flung family,
walk into the house
for the first time
and within ten
minutes, fall down
the basement steps
and knock his noggin,
then, before anyone
can get a good
look at him and
invoke the concussion
watch, run howling
upstairs and lock him-
self in the bathroom?

O the exasperated
calm of his mother
on her knees in the hall
by the keyhole! O
the swagger of his father
positioning the ladder
ascending with all

the confidence of a
Miami drug salesman
only to find the window
painted shut.

Cliff

This is the poem I don't want to write, you
don't want to read. OK. I won't if you won't.
But look, here's the next line. We're dangling
over this cliff of white space. We've got to find
a foothold and climb down. Think. Stay in
your body. Where is your left foot? Feel for
a notch. There, now your right. Now lower
your left hand. Lean in. Hug the rock with
your whole self. Say, if I fall it will be toward
this rocky breast which will hold me. Not
down to death. Now. Move your right hand.

I don't have to write the details: Gold
sweater, gold, brown and green checked
corduroy skirt. The morning after the night
in the bathroom. Blood blooming through
bandages under my sleeves. The principal
calling my mother. I don't have to write
right hand on the razor blade, scarlet
ribbons flowing from my left wrist. Did
we have that album yet, Harry Belafonte,
*As for me, some scarlet ribbons, scarlet
ribbons for my hair?* Then the left hand
works at the right wrist's under-skin
river. Both hands panic at the blood. I
will stain things, get caught. This will
kill my parents. Blood draws me out
of the miserable cell of myself into

the upstairs bathroom where pink
water cools in the tub and the muffled
croon of Daddy's radio fills the silence
between snores. If I die, they will still
be here, stuck with what's left. No way
to disappear like I wanted, to escape
the dark weight my life has become.
What is wrong with me? Thirteen years
old, I don't have a clue. But at the bottom
of that cliff a five-year-old is waiting.
She will wait another forty years.

Yard

D-Day

Probably the nasturtiums,
whose stems and leaves
she tossed in salads
for a peppery bite,
were in bloom
in the garden
next to the hedge
that June morning
when she heard the news
as she left the kitchen
and went out
with her basket of wash.

Seeing her neighbor,
old as her mother,
hanging out clothes
in her yard, too,
Mother called across
the hedge: "Mrs. Mac,
have you heard?
Our troops have landed!
The invasion has begun!"

At word of this mission
to free the world
from tyranny

Mrs. Mac replied,
"I can't wait for Joe
to come home
and turn on the radio."

Westward Ho

When Mother looked under
the sheet we'd put over
the picnic table

and found Warren and me
playing covered wagon
she would have hit the ceiling

had the back yard had one
not because we were exploring
how the prairie got populated—

we weren't—but because we'd
opened cans of corn and chili
taken without asking

in order to provide
our imaginary selves
with real pioneer food.

At Play

All I remember about playing
King of the Hill on the slight slope
in the front yard is that one person
was king and everybody else tried
to drag her down. No brains, no
allowances for size or age, no fairness
in numbers. Every King of the Hill
was summarily toppled. The harder
you fought the more likely you were
to win gouges and contusions. You
attained your height, trumpeted
"I'm King of the Hill!" and then
the dogs were on you: Paula, all long
knobby bones; PJ, dense as a bowling
ball; Cathy, whose blond mane might
blind you as her long nails raked
your back; and Susan, whose specialty
was head butts under the chin. This
was blood sport, this melee by
the boxwoods out of which came
a new king we cheered, then conquered.

All of It

Postgraduate Work

I am the one who, thirty years ago,
wanted to write a dissertation on
The House as the Body in the Work
of Four American Women Poets.
I saw then, in the joists and plumbing
of poems, this primal link. I understood
it with the three pounds of electric jelly
that was my brain. I read, researched,
proposed, was refused, and took off
down another path.
                                    Now I'm back
in that thorny clearing. I don't need
brains to see it. The punch to the solar
plexus, the knot in the gut as I step
into a house slowing down around
her. It is immaterial that the cleaning
lady comes once a week. Outside energy
can't travel across the placenta; she
can tidy but not animate the house.
Mother's vitality kept the air alive,
circulating like hot water when we had
steam heat. A house is a child you carry
on the outside. As you go, it goes. It's
dizzy. It can't breathe. Can't look sharp.
Can't get its shit together or in the pot.
Can't regulate what comes in, what goes
out. Can't fix what breaks. Can't even find
it. And I can't tell the living from the ghosts.

It Doesn't Matter

that she is too weak
to open the car door,
she is going to work.

When she can't turn
the key, she says the fault
is in the ignition.

She's never had a car
act like this before.
They don't make them

like they used to.

In the ER

All I see is You
on the gurney
in your purple
nightgown

Six hours I sit
holding your
hand, the dark
searchlight

of Your eye
scouring
my brainpan
my heart

for what this
means: Face
twisted, no
voice   Pressure
in your

inner river
surging:
Hold me fast
to some
Truth before
they cut

this nightgown
off   Before
nurses slide me
bed to board

before flight
crew straps
Me down

Keep your hand
pulse to Pulse in
mine till we
know some-
Thing, make some-
Thing of my
eighty-nine
years

On Her Side

When I told the healer about my mother's last day—
the stroke, no neurologist to give the clot-dissolving shot;
mountains fogged in, no airlift possible; no ambulance
for long-distance transport

when I told her of my frantic drive back, cell service
disappearing in road cuts, around hills, trying to talk
to the ER doctor whose true language was Hindi,
trying to talk to my brother in Ireland

when I wept and said storms next morning kept
the helicopter away till noon; then I chased it back
to Lexington to find Mother in another ER, on a ventilator,
how they couldn't do more tests because something seemed
to be happening
                                    more strokes
                heart stopped
                                                    CODE
        shocked twice
                                a mountain range of beats

when I said, after doctor talks and more phone calls, I told
them not to start my mother's heart again

        and my husband and sons and girlfriend gathered
        round

then stepped out

and with just me
                          holding her hand
    life left

    twenty-four hours after she
    was carried from her house

the healer said

"Everything was on her side."

Final Play

Her grandkids
called her GG
for Glad Granny.

At the funeral home
my son slipped
those Scrabble tiles
into the box.

Labor

I am doggedly working
at what I do not want to see happen:
    removing everything she chose
    scouring every handprint.
It's my job
    to render these rooms,
    the signature of her life,
    anonymous;
get down to the bare space
Papaw built
for her and Daddy to move into.

What was it like that day?
Another question
I never thought to ask.

No matter now.
However it began, her life
in this house is complete.
So mine must be too
except for this

                sorting

                      pitching

                            carrying away.

Every Cupboard Bare,
Every Head Bowed

Loading the truck for the last leaving
we moved Granny Buby's table
away from the wall where it had stood
since her death the month Armstrong
walked on the moon. I was done
sorting through, emptying out.
All the lost was lost, the found found,

till the table top
                                swiveled
revealing, in secret space,
a leather pouch

of deeds   summonses
                ration coupons
Daddy's will when arthritis hit,
ticket stubs (baseball, Coney Island)
stock in
                what no longer exists,
papers making Papaw guardian
of his dead brother's
child
                                        (what child?)

a ballet (ballad) hand-writ in amber ink

a newspaper clipping:

My brother **WINS BEE THOUGH ILL**
the bill for our '55 Ford,
and another, dated 1906,
for repairs on Papaw's daddy's
two-horse wagon.

Thanksgiving Night

After I'd locked
the house
for the last time
I kissed the door.

Now, remembering,
I feel my lips
on my breastbone.

The Day After

I wake up and the house I just took
apart has reassembled in my mind.

The hall carpet is that flat-nap green
with darker green swirl from I don't know
how long ago. The whatnot anchors
the corner at the foot of the stairs
where the grandfather clock stood
for thirty years. Time has come
loose, like the objects themselves.
Freed from the last place Mother left
them, they've sought out snug pockets
of memory. The washer and dryer have
appeared from behind louvered doors
and occupied the end of the kitchen
beneath the yellow and white clock
and copper chafing dishes I packed away
yesterday. Tomorrow the washer may be
back in the basement, and the dryer, four
wires between clothesline poles.

The kitchen is blue or covered in parchment-
hued wallpaper laced with fine-drawn leaves.
The spinet is back and the oval-framed prints
of elegant ladies I pretended were our kin.
It's Christmas. It's June and we're having a fish fry

in the backyard. I'm ten, posing with my new bike
and birthday guests. My teacher came!

She brought chicken salad after Mother died.
I'm up with a newborn in the middle of the night.
It's untelling what chair I'll find to sit in, what
room, what year. The dead are here
with that tacked-down ripped-out
carpet. Coffee's brewing in the percolator,
the vacuum pot, the Braun. We'll
eat from empty cupboards
on auctioned china. All the gone
clocks tell different times.

I Can't Believe

that I gave away _____
that I left _____
that I kept _____

I can't believe nobody wanted _____
or fought over _____
or asked about _____

all those _____
all that _____
that he collected
that she polished
that framed their life

I can't believe the boxes
I carried in
and taped together
and filled
and carried out

clothes
      dishes
           books
                  figurines
            coins
     clocks

every item
in every drawer
or cupboard
or bookcase

on every shelf
in every closet
went through my hands

bent on taking apart
what my parents
put together
their home
inside the house
Papaw built

Welcome

Late afternoon I lie down for a nap but instead of sleep Daddy
opens the door behind my eyes. He's in his shirtsleeves standing on
the carpet before the carpet before the flood. He reaches me into a hug
snug as bark. "I didn't think you were here," I say. "Yep," he answers. "It's
me." "But Daddy," I start, "it's all gone." Nonsense. How can the house
be gone when we're standing in it? "What time is it?" I ask and he laughs.
No time, no time at all.

In memory of my parents
and in thanksgiving for our life
in the many-storied house

Acknowledgments

Many-Storied House could not have been written without support from

- my writers' group (Marie Bradby, Janece Walters-Cook, Martha Gehringer, Leatha Kendrick, Lou Martin, and Ann Olson);
- Sandy Ballard, Joan Hoskins, Pat Hudson, Roberta White, and Steve Lyon, who read for me;
- poets Richard Taylor and Lisa Williams, who critiqued the manuscript for the University Press of Kentucky;
- the Appalachian Writers Workshop at Hindman Settlement School;
- the Hambidge Center for the Arts;
- folks who came to readings and asked, "When are those poems going to be in a book?"
- and my students far and wide whose energy and intent nurture mine as we write together.

My thanks to Robert Easley for allowing a photo of his painting to be used on page 2;

to Ken Davis at Staples;

and to Ashley Runyon, Iris Law, Deborah Golden, and everyone at the University Press of Kentucky for believing in this book and working to make it happen.

I am also grateful to the editors of the following publications where these poems, in slightly different versions, appeared:

Appalachian Journal, "Art," "Money Laundering," and "Labor"; *Art in Kentucky,* "With a Song in His Heart"; *For All Our Voices,* "Provenance"; *Jelly Bucket Literary Review,* "Postgraduate Work"; *Pine Mountain Sand and Gravel,* "Smithereens."

Index of First Lines

Kentucky Voices

Miss America Kissed Caleb
Billy C. Clark

New Covenant Bound
T. Crunk

The Total Light Process: New and Selected Poems
James Baker Hall

Upheaval: Stories
Chris Holbrook

Appalachian Elegy
bell hooks

Many-Storied House: Poems
George Ella Lyon

With a Hammer for My Heart: A Novel
George Ella Lyon

Famous People I Have Known
Ed McClanahan

Nothing Like an Ocean: Stories
Jim Tomlinson

Sue Mundy: A Novel of the Civil War
Richard Taylor

At The Breakers: A Novel
Mary Ann Taylor-Hall

Come and Go, Molly Snow: A Novel
Mary Ann Taylor-Hall

Buffalo Dance: The Journey of York
Frank X Walker

When Winter Come: The Ascension of York
Frank X Walker

The Cave
Robert Penn Warren